Seeing the small is called Clarity. Keeping flexible is called Strength.
Using the shining Radiance you enter the Light, where no harm
can come to you. This is called Enlightenment.

– Lao Tsu

If you open yourself to insight,
you are at one with insight
and you can use it completely.

– Lao Tsu

Leaning alone in the close bamboo,
I am playing a lute and humming a song too softly
for anyone to hear — except my comrade, the bright moon.

– Wang Wei

I know within my heart what is good
and what is beautiful.

- Wang Wei

Express yourself completely, then become quiet.
Open yourself to heaven and earth, then trust your
natural responses; everything will fall into place.

– Lao Tsu

Serenity is yours. When chaos looms,
seek the surrender of sweet simplicity.

- Ching Qu Lam

I take into my being all that I see and hear,
soothing my senses, quieting my heart.

- Qiu Wei

Flow with what is happening and let your mind be free.
Find the center through pure acceptance.

- Chuang Tzu

Seeing the small is called Clarity. Keeping flexible is called Strength.
Using the shining Radiance you enter the Light, where no harm
can come to you. This is called Enlightenment.

– Lao Tsu

If you open yourself to insight,
you are at one with insight
and you can use it completely.

– Lao Tsu

Leaning alone in the close bamboo,
I am playing a lute and humming a song too softly
for anyone to hear — except my comrade, the bright moon.

– Wang Wei

I know within my heart what is good
and what is beautiful.

- Wang Wei

Express yourself completely, then become quiet.
Open yourself to heaven and earth, then trust your
natural responses; everything will fall into place.

- Lao Tsu

Serenity is yours. When chaos looms,
seek the surrender of sweet simplicity.

- Ching Qu Lam

I take into my being all that I see and hear,
soothing my senses, quieting my heart.

– Qiu Wei

Flow with what is happening and let your mind be free.
Find the center through pure acceptance.

- Chuang Tzu

Seeing the small is called Clarity. Keeping flexible is called Strength.
Using the shining Radiance you enter the Light, where no harm
can come to you. This is called Enlightenment.

– Lao Tsu

If you open yourself to insight,
you are at one with insight
and you can use it completely.

– Lao Tsu

Leaning alone in the close bamboo,
I am playing a lute and humming a song too softly
for anyone to hear — except my comrade, the bright moon.

- Wang Wei

I know within my heart what is good
and what is beautiful.

- Wang Wei

Express yourself completely, then become quiet.
Open yourself to heaven and earth, then trust your
natural responses; everything will fall into place.

- Lao Tsu

Serenity is yours. When chaos looms,
seek the surrender of sweet simplicity.

- Ching Qu Lam

I take into my being all that I see and hear,
soothing my senses, quieting my heart.

– Qiu Wei

Flow with what is happening and let your mind be free.
Find the center through pure acceptance.

- Chuang Tzu

Seeing the small is called Clarity. Keeping flexible is called Strength.
Using the shining Radiance you enter the Light, where no harm
can come to you. This is called Enlightenment.

– Lao Tsu

If you open yourself to insight,
you are at one with insight
and you can use it completely.

- Lao Tsu

Leaning alone in the close bamboo,
I am playing a lute and humming a song too softly
for anyone to hear — except my comrade, the bright moon.

- Wang Wei

I know within my heart what is good
and what is beautiful.

- Wang Wei

Express yourself completely, then become quiet.
Open yourself to heaven and earth, then trust your
natural responses; everything will fall into place.

– Lao Tsu

Serenity is yours. When chaos looms,
seek the surrender of sweet simplicity.

- Ching Qu Lam

I take into my being all that I see and hear,
soothing my senses, quieting my heart.

– Qiu Wei

Flow with what is happening and let your mind be free.
Find the center through pure acceptance.

- Chuang Tzu

Seeing the small is called Clarity. Keeping flexible is called Strength.
Using the shining Radiance you enter the Light, where no harm
can come to you. This is called Enlightenment.

– Lao Tsu

If you open yourself to insight,
you are at one with insight
and you can use it completely.

- Lao Tsu

Leaning alone in the close bamboo,
I am playing a lute and humming a song too softly
for anyone to hear — except my comrade, the bright moon.

– Wang Wei

I know within my heart what is good
and what is beautiful.

- Wang Wei

Express yourself completely, then become quiet.
Open yourself to heaven and earth, then trust your
natural responses; everything will fall into place.

– Lao Tsu

Serenity is yours. When chaos looms,
seek the surrender of sweet simplicity.

- Ching Qu Lam

I take into my being all that I see and hear,
soothing my senses, quieting my heart.

- Qiu Wei

Flow with what is happening and let your mind be free.
Find the center through pure acceptance.

- Chuang Tzu

Seeing the small is called Clarity. Keeping flexible is called Strength.
Using the shining Radiance you enter the Light, where no harm
can come to you. This is called Enlightenment.

– Lao Tsu

If you open yourself to insight,
you are at one with insight
and you can use it completely.

– Lao Tsu

Leaning alone in the close bamboo,
I am playing a lute and humming a song too softly
for anyone to hear — except my comrade, the bright moon.

- Wang Wei

I know within my heart what is good
and what is beautiful.

– Wang Wei

Express yourself completely, then become quiet.
Open yourself to heaven and earth, then trust your
natural responses; everything will fall into place.

– Lao Tsu

Serenity is yours. When chaos looms,
seek the surrender of sweet simplicity.

- Ching Qu Lam

I take into my being all that I see and hear,
soothing my senses, quieting my heart.

- Qiu Wei

Flow with what is happening and let your mind be free.
Find the center through pure acceptance.

– Chuang Tzu

Seeing the small is called Clarity. Keeping flexible is called Strength.
Using the shining Radiance you enter the Light, where no harm
can come to you. This is called Enlightenment.

– Lao Tsu

If you open yourself to insight,
you are at one with insight
and you can use it completely.

– Lao Tsu

Leaning alone in the close bamboo,
I am playing a lute and humming a song too softly
for anyone to hear — except my comrade, the bright moon.

– Wang Wei

I know within my heart what is good
and what is beautiful.

- Wang Wei

Express yourself completely, then become quiet.
Open yourself to heaven and earth, then trust your
natural responses; everything will fall into place.

– Lao Tsu

Serenity is yours. When chaos looms,
seek the surrender of sweet simplicity.

- Ching Qu Lam

I take into my being all that I see and hear,
soothing my senses, quieting my heart.

— Qiu Wei

Flow with what is happening and let your mind be free.
Find the center through pure acceptance.

- Chuang Tzu

Seeing the small is called Clarity. Keeping flexible is called Strength.
Using the shining Radiance you enter the Light, where no harm
can come to you. This is called Enlightenment.

– Lao Tsu

If you open yourself to insight,
you are at one with insight
and you can use it completely.

– Lao Tsu

Leaning alone in the close bamboo,
I am playing a lute and humming a song too softly
for anyone to hear — except my comrade, the bright moon.

- Wang Wei

I know within my heart what is good
and what is beautiful.

– Wang Wei

Express yourself completely, then become quiet.
Open yourself to heaven and earth, then trust your
natural responses; everything will fall into place.

– Lao Tsu

Serenity is yours. When chaos looms,
seek the surrender of sweet simplicity.

- Ching Qu Lam

I take into my being all that I see and hear,
soothing my senses, quieting my heart.

– Qiu Wei

Flow with what is happening and let your mind be free.
Find the center through pure acceptance.

- Chuang Tzu

Seeing the small is called Clarity. Keeping flexible is called Strength.
Using the shining Radiance you enter the Light, where no harm
can come to you. This is called Enlightenment.

– Lao Tsu

If you open yourself to insight,
you are at one with insight
and you can use it completely.

- Lao Tsu

Leaning alone in the close bamboo,
I am playing a lute and humming a song too softly
for anyone to hear — except my comrade, the bright moon.

– Wang Wei

I know within my heart what is good
and what is beautiful.

- Wang Wei

Express yourself completely, then become quiet.
Open yourself to heaven and earth, then trust your
natural responses; everything will fall into place.

- Lao Tsu

Serenity is yours. When chaos looms,
seek the surrender of sweet simplicity.

- Ching Qu Lam

I take into my being all that I see and hear,
soothing my senses, quieting my heart.

- Qiu Wei

Flow with what is happening and let your mind be free.
Find the center through pure acceptance.

– Chuang Tzu

Seeing the small is called Clarity. Keeping flexible is called Strength.
Using the shining Radiance you enter the Light, where no harm
can come to you. This is called Enlightenment.

– Lao Tsu

If you open yourself to insight,
you are at one with insight
and you can use it completely.

– Lao Tsu

Leaning alone in the close bamboo,
I am playing a lute and humming a song too softly
for anyone to hear — except my comrade, the bright moon.

– Wang Wei

I know within my heart what is good
and what is beautiful.

– Wang Wei

Express yourself completely, then become quiet.
Open yourself to heaven and earth, then trust your
natural responses; everything will fall into place.

– Lao Tsu

Serenity is yours. When chaos looms,
seek the surrender of sweet simplicity.

- Ching Qu Lam

I take into my being all that I see and hear,
soothing my senses, quieting my heart.

- Qiu Wei

Flow with what is happening and let your mind be free.
Find the center through pure acceptance.

- Chuang Tzu

Seeing the small is called Clarity. Keeping flexible is called Strength.
Using the shining Radiance you enter the Light, where no harm
can come to you. This is called Enlightenment.

– Lao Tsu

If you open yourself to insight,
you are at one with insight
and you can use it completely.

– Lao Tsu

Leaning alone in the close bamboo,
I am playing a lute and humming a song too softly
for anyone to hear — except my comrade, the bright moon.

– Wang Wei

I know within my heart what is good
and what is beautiful.

- Wang Wei

Express yourself completely, then become quiet.
Open yourself to heaven and earth, then trust your
natural responses; everything will fall into place.

– Lao Tsu

Serenity is yours. When chaos looms,
seek the surrender of sweet simplicity.

- Ching Qu Lam

I take into my being all that I see and hear,
soothing my senses, quieting my heart.

– Qiu Wei

Flow with what is happening and let your mind be free.
Find the center through pure acceptance.

- Chuang Tzu

Seeing the small is called Clarity. Keeping flexible is called Strength.
Using the shining Radiance you enter the Light, where no harm
can come to you. This is called Enlightenment.

– Lao Tsu

If you open yourself to insight,
you are at one with insight
and you can use it completely.

– Lao Tsu

Leaning alone in the close bamboo,
I am playing a lute and humming a song too softly
for anyone to hear — except my comrade, the bright moon.

- Wang Wei

I know within my heart what is good
and what is beautiful.

- Wang Wei

Express yourself completely, then become quiet.
Open yourself to heaven and earth, then trust your
natural responses; everything will fall into place.

- Lao Tsu

Serenity is yours. When chaos looms,
seek the surrender of sweet simplicity.

- Ching Qu Lam

I take into my being all that I see and hear,
soothing my senses, quieting my heart.

– Qiu Wei

Flow with what is happening and let your mind be free.
Find the center through pure acceptance.

- Chuang Tzu